I ♥ My Future HBCU

Teaching Children About Historically Black Colleges & Universities

By Nathalie Nelson Parker

TO: _____

FROM: _____

I LOVE MY FUTURE MY HBCU

Copyright © 2019 by By Nathalie Nelson Parker. All rights reserved.

All rights reserved. Printed in the United States of America. No part of this book may be used or reproduced in any manner whatsoever without written permission except in the case of brief quotations embodied in critical articles or reviews.

ISBN: 978-1-7358233-9-3

Printed in the United States of America

Dedication

To my mom, thank you for teaching me the value of education.

To my husband, our HBCU love story inspires me everyday.

To my son, thank you for all the ways you empower me to explore and imagine.

Special thanks to my HBCU All-Star family, and all persons who invest in our HBCU's everyday; thank you for all that you do.

Finally, to the beautiful children and families that may read this book, I hope one day you will love your future HBCU too.

Love, Nathalie

Madison and LJ walk into the kitchen. They take their normal seats around the kitchen counter for breakfast. Mom and Dad are busy cooking a delicious meal.

"Come on Madison and LJ," mom calls. "Eat up!"

Madison and LJ grab their forks. LJ turns to his sister. "Hey, what's that on mommy's shirt?"

"I don't know," Madison states. "Mommy, what is an *HBCU*?"

"Well, Madison," mom replies. "An *HBCU* is a historically black college or university."

"What's the difference between an *HBCU* and other colleges?" LJ asks.

"It's just as great as other colleges and universities but with more soul!" exclaims dad.

"More soul?" LJ and Madison ask as they turn to each other.

"Yes, more soul. Let me show you," mom says.

Dad grabs mom's hand and the family is immediately transported to the beautiful campus of Memory Lane.

"*HBCUs* have so much soul," mom explains.

"See," dad points to the right. "There are marching bands."

Mom points to the left. "And don't forget about the dance and step teams."

"That's right," dad says. "Oh and also fraternities and sororities."

"What is that?" LJ asks excitedly.

"It's like having a lot of brothers and sisters."

"Like a really big family?" LJ inquires.

"That's right," mom replies. "So cool," Madison and LJ say together.

As Madison and LJ continue to walk the campus of Memory Lane they are filled with joy. The air is filled with so many exciting sounds of beautiful music and the laughter of friends.

"Look!" mom exclaims. "There are even kings and queens."

"Wow!" Madison shouts. "When I grow up, I want to be a queen too."

"You will be princess," dad says kissing her hand.

"Did you know celebrities, doctors, lawyers, teachers and many other great people attended *HBCUs*?" mom adds.

Madison and LJ look at each other amazed. "Wow!" they shout.

"Plus, *HBCUs* have history," dad shares.

"History?" Madison questions. "What kind of history?"

Mom, dad, LJ and Madison all sit down on a bench overlooking the president's house near the lake.

"Our ancestors, unlike you and me, could not choose the schools they wanted to attend," dad continues.

"Why not?" LJ asks with confusion.

"They could only go to the schools made for African Americans. Many of these schools are still around. That is why we call them *HBCUs* or historically black colleges and universities."

"Wow!" Madison says with a smile. "I want to go to an *HBCU*." "Me too, me too!" says LJ raising his hand.

"You sure can," mom says with pride. "In the future, when you finish high school."

"Did you know when you go to an *HBCU* you will learn to walk tall? Mom asks.

LJ and Madison stand up straight and cross their arms around their chest.

"Have pride!" mom exclaims. "And be the best young man and woman you can be."

Madison and LJ smile as mom pats them on the head.

"Really?" They ask in unison.

"Yes," dad says. "Mom and I learned that at our *HBCU*, and that's where we met too." Mom and dad look at each other lovingly.

Dad continues, "You will learn how to improve your community and even the world."

"Well mommy, I love my future *HBCU*!" Madison exclaims.

"Me too daddy! I love my future *HBCU* too." LJ says with pride.

Dad wraps both children in his arms while holding the hand of his wife. "We love our *HBCU*, and we love you too!"

The End

White House Initiative on Historically Black Colleges and Universities School Directory

Alabama A & M University,
Normal, AL
www.aamu.edu

Alabama State University,
Montgomery, AL
www.alasu.edu

Albany State University, Albany, GA
www.asurams.edu

Alcorn State University,
Alcorn State, MS
www.alcorn.edu

Allen University, Columbia, SC
allenuniversity.edu

Arkansas Baptist College,
Little Rock, AR
www.arkansasbaptist.edu

Benedict College, Columbia, SC
www.benedict.edu

Bennett College, Greensboro, NC
www.bennett.edu

Bethune-Cookman University,
Daytona Beach, FL
www.cookman.edu

Bishop State Community College,
Mobile, AL
www.bishop.edu

Bluefield State College, Bluefield, WV
www.bluefieldstate.edu

Bowie State University, Bowie, MD
www.bowiestate.edu

Central State University, Wilberforce, OH
www.centralstate.edu

Cheyney University of Pennsylvania, Cheyney, PA
www.cheyney.edu

Claflin University, Orangeburg, SC
www.claflin.edu

Clark Atlanta University, Atlanta, GA
www.cau.edu

Clinton College, Rock Hill, SC
www.clintonjuniorcollege.edu

Coahoma Community College, Clarksdale, MS
www.coahomacc.edu

Concordia College Alabama, Selma, AL
www.ccal.edu

Coppin State University, Baltimore, MD
www.coppin.edu

Delaware State University, Dover, DE
www.desu.edu

Denmark Technical College, Denmark, SC
www.denmarktech.edu

Dillard University, New Orleans, LA
www.dillard.edu

Edward Waters College, Jacksonville, FL
www.ewc.edu

Elizabeth City State University, Elizabeth City, NC
www.ecsu.edu

Fayetteville State University, Fayetteville, NC
www.uncfsu.edu

Fisk University, Nashville, TN
www.fisk.edu

Florida Agricultural and Mechanical University, Tallahassee, FL
www.famu.edu

Florida Memorial University,
Miami Gardens, FL
www.fmuniv.edu

Fort Valley State University,
Fort Valley, GA
www.fvsu.edu

Gadsden State Community College,
Gadsden, AL
www.gadsdenstate.edu

Grambling State University,
Grambling, LA
www.gram.edu

H Councill Trenholm State Technical
College, Montgomery, AL
www.trenholmstate.edu

Hampton University, Hampton, VA
www.hamptonu.edu

Harris-Stowe State University,
Saint Louis, MO
www.hssu.edu

Howard University, Washington, DC
www.howard.edu

Huston-Tillotson University, Austin, TX
www.htu.edu

Interdenominational Theological Center,
Atlanta, GA
www.itc.edu

J.F. Drake State Community and
Technical College, Huntsville, AL
www.drakestate.edu

Jackson State University, Jackson, MS
www.jsums.edu

Jarvis Christian College, Hawkins, TX
www.jarvis.edu

Johnson C Smith University,
Charlotte, NC
www.jcsu.edu

Kentucky State University, Frankfort, KY
www.kysu.edu

Lane College, Jackson, TN
www.lanecollege.edu

Langston University, Langston, OK
www.lunet.edu

Lawson State Community College-
Birmingham Campus, Birmingham, AL
www.lawsonstate.edu

Le Moyne-Owen College, Memphis, TN
www.loc.edu

Lincoln University, Jefferson City, MO
www.lincolnu.edu

Lincoln University of Pennsylvania,
Lincoln University, PA
www.lincoln.edu

Livingstone College, Salisbury, NC
www.livingstone.edu

Meharry Medical College, Nashville, TN
www.mmc.edu

Miles College, Fairfield, AL
www.miles.edu

Mississippi Valley State University,
Itta Bena, MS
www.mvsu.edu

Morehouse College, Atlanta, GA
www.morehouse.edu

Morehouse School of Medicine,
Atlanta, GA
www.msm.edu

Morgan State University, Baltimore, MD
www.morgan.edu

Morris College, Sumter, SC
www.morris.edu

Norfolk State University, Norfolk, VA
www.nsu.edu

North Carolina A & T State University,
Greensboro, NC
www.ncat.edu

North Carolina Central University,
Durham, NC
www.nccu.edu

Oakwood University, Huntsville, AL
www.oakwood.edu

Paine College, Augusta, GA
www.paine.edu

Paul Quinn College, Dallas, TX
www.pqc.edu

Philander Smith College,
Little Rock, AR
www.philander.edu

Prairie View A & M University,
Prairie View, TX
www.pvamu.edu

Rust College, Holly Springs, MS
www.rustcollege.edu

Saint Augustine's University,
Raleigh, NC
www.st-aug.edu

Savannah State University,
Savannah, GA
www.savannahstate.edu

Selma University, Selma, AL
selmauniversity.org

Shaw University, Raleigh, NC
www.shawuniversity.edu

Shelton State Community College,
Tuscaloosa, AL
www.sheltonstate.edu

Shorter College, N Little Rock, AR
www.shortercollege.org

South Carolina State University,
Orangeburg, SC
www.scsu.edu

Southern University and A & M
College, Baton Rouge, LA
www.subr.edu

Southern University at New Orleans,
New Orleans, LA
www.suno.edu

Southern University at Shreveport,
Shreveport, LA
www.susla.edu

Southwestern Christian College,
Terrell, TX
www.swcc.edu

Spelman College, Atlanta, GA
www.spelman.edu

St Philip's College, San Antonio, TX
www.alamo.edu

Stillman College, Tuscaloosa, AL
www.stillman.edu

Talladega College, Talladega, AL
www.talladega.edu

Tennessee State University, Nashville, TN
www.tnstate.edu

Texas College, Tyler, TX
www.texascollege.edu

Texas Southern University,
Houston, TX
www.tsu.edu

Tougaloo College, Tougaloo, MS
www.tougaloo.edu

Tuskegee University, Tuskegee, AL
www.tuskegee.edu

University of Arkansas at Pine Bluff,
Pine Bluff, AR
www.uapb.edu

University of Maryland Eastern Shore,
Princess Anne, MD
www.umes.edu

University of the District of Columbia,
Washington, DC
www.udc.edu

University of the Virgin Islands,
Charlotte Amalie, VI
www.uvi.edu

Virginia State University,
Petersburg, VA
www.vsu.edu

Virginia Union University,
Richmond, VA
www.vuu.edu

Virginia University of Lynchburg,
Lynchburg, VA
www.vul.edu

Voorhees College, Denmark, SC
www.voorhees.edu

West Virginia State University,
Institute, WV
www.wvstateu.edu

Wilberforce University,
Wilberforce, OH
www.wilberforce.edu

Wiley College, Marshall, TX
wileyc.edu

Winston-Salem State University,
Winston- Salem, NC
www.wssu.edu

Xavier University of Louisiana,
New Orleans, LA
www.xula.edu

*White House Initiative on Historically Black Colleges and Universities School Directory. Retrieved from http://sites.ed.gov/whhbcu/

www.ingramcontent.com/pod-product-compliance
Lightning Source LLC
Chambersburg PA
CBHW051306110526
44589CB00025B/2948